THE PALOMINO HORSE

by Gail B. Stewart

Illustrated with photographs
by William Muñoz

Capstone Press

MINNEAPOLIS

Printed in the United States of America.

Capstone Press • 2440 Fernbrook Lane • Minneapolis, MN 55447

Editorial Director   John Coughlan
Managing Editor   Tom Streissguth
Production Editor   James Stapleton
Book Design   Timothy Halldin

Library of Congress Cataloging in Publication Data

Stewart, Gail, 1949-
    The palomino horse / Gail B. Stewart ; illustrated with photographs by William Muñoz.
        p. cm.
    Includes bibliographical references (p. 44) and index.
    Summary: Discusses the history, physical characteristics, and uses of the horses known for their unique gold coloration and white mane and tail.
    ISBN 1-56065-299-3
    1. Palomino horse--Juvenile literature. [1. Palomino horse. 2. Horses.] I. Muñoz, William, ill. II. Title.
    SF293.P3S74 1996
    636.1'3--dc20   95-11256
                                                              CIP
                                                              AC

Table of Contents

Quick Facts about Palominos

Description

Height: 14.1 to 16 **hands** (equal to four-inch [ten-centimeter] segments) from the **withers** (the top of the shoulders). That works out to between 56 and 64 inches (142 to 162 centimeters) tall.

Weight:	approximately 1100 pounds (500 kilograms)
Features:	Palominos are a color type. They have a golden coat, white mane, and a white tail. They may also have white patches on their face and on their legs below the knees.

Range

western North America

Uses

Palominos are used for ranching, rodeos, pleasure riding, trail rides, and parades.

Chapter 1

The Golden Ones

Some people have called them "magical horses." Some saw them as bad luck, while others saw them as a blessing from the gods. They are easy to spot, even by people who do not know very much about horses.

"I think a Palomino was the first horse I ever saw," says one fan. "I used to love going to the movies and seeing cowboys on the screen. The good guys, at least the ones I liked best, rode Palominos. That was the kind of horse I always wanted to ride."

It is easy to recognize a Palomino. Its coat shines brightly, and its mane and tail are pure white. And Palominos always carry themselves proudly.

"I believe they know how beautiful they are," says a horse breeder. "They toss those white manes and pick up their feet as if they were dancing. There is nothing like the sight of a Palomino racing as fast as it can go."

A Mysterious Horse

Palominos are a little mysterious. No one can predict when a Palomino will be born, because two Palomino parents do not necessarily produce a Palomino **foal** (baby horse). The Palomino is rare, and that is one of the reasons it is so valuable.

Palominos gallop through a grassy corral.

A Palomino is a horse of a different color—and it is impossible to predict when one will be born.

"I used to think it would be great to know which parents would have a young Palomino," one horse breeder says. "Now I'm not so sure. They are rare and unexpected, and that makes Palominos a wonderful surprise."

What is the background of the Palomino? Why is its color so rare? Why have Palominos been looked at in a special way over the centuries? And how are Palominos used today?

Chapter 2

A Horse from Ancient Times

People never used the term "Palomino" before 1920. Because the word is modern, some people believe that the Palomino is a new horse. Experts disagree. The word may be new, they say, but the Palomino horse has been around since ancient times.

Palominos in Myth and Legend

More than 1,000 years ago, the ancient Greeks told stories about their heroes, gods, and goddesses. One famous Greek hero was

Achilles, who was given two magical horses named Balios and Xanthos. They could outrun any other horse and were smarter than most humans. Horse experts believe these horses may have been Palominos.

According to legend, Balios and Xanthos had a color like that of old gold. Their long manes and tails were like silk and sparkled like sunbeams.

A light tan Palomino blends in with its snowy surroundings.

In the myths of the ancient Scandinavians, the gods and goddesses rode beautiful horses with golden coats and snow-white manes and tails. The horses had names like Gull Toppr (gold top) and Gisl (sunbeam).

The Bad Luck Horse

Palominos were not always linked with gods and heroes. Sometimes the horses were bad luck, as in one ancient legend from Scotland.

In this story, two men decided to go fishing, instead of attending church, on a Sunday. One of the men spied a golden horse with a white mane in a nearby field. He jumped on its back, even though the other man warned him that the horse was really the devil in disguise. The horse dashed away, and neither the man nor the golden horse was ever seen again.

Palominos in Art

Artists have long admired the beauty of golden horses. There are Palominos in ancient paintings from China, Persia, and Japan. The portraits of many famous generals and soldiers show them sitting on the backs of Palominos.

Artists have also painted knights in armor on the backs of Palominos. Like modern draft horses, these horses were large and muscular. They had to carry hundreds of pounds of metal armor as well as the heavy weapons used in those days.

Palominos appear in a rare and beautiful cloth known as the Bayeux Tapestry. This work was created in France almost 900 years ago. It shows many horses, but the most striking are the golden horses with white manes and tails.

Chapter 3

The Palomino Comes to America

When people think of Palominos, they think of the American West. Palominos are often seen in Texas, Arizona, and California. For that reason, people mistakenly believe that they are native to the United States. Actually, no horse is native to the United States.

Their unusual coloring makes Palominos rare and valuable horses.

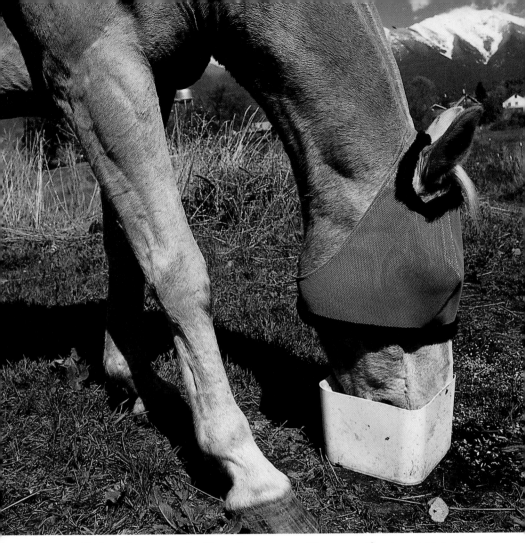

Palominos and other horses will sometimes wear a mask to stay warm in cold, windy weather.

Brought From Europe

Modern horses of the United States and Canada descend from European horses. In the

16th century, explorers from Spain arrived in North America. They knew there were no horses in the New World, so they brought their own.

The Spanish used their horses for transportation and for herding cattle on large ranches. They also found them useful in fighting the Native Americans.

Over time, other people brought their horses to America from Europe. Each country had its own kind of horse. Many of the English horses were tall, long-legged, and fast. Spanish horses were often strong and muscular.

Horse owners carefully bred different types of horses. They hoped that the new foals would have the best characteristics of each parent. In many cases, this is exactly what happened. Soon there were horses that had the speed of the English horses, with the agility and strength of the Spanish breeds.

Settling the West

The prairies of North America were perfect for raising horses. There was plenty of grass for grazing and cold, clear water for drinking. The endless miles of open land gave the horses lots of running room, too.

The horses that roamed these prairies were of many different colors. Some were jet black, and others were white. There were many shades of brown and gray. And some horses had golden coats with white manes and tails. These horses would later be called Palominos.

Settlers used these horses in their daily work. They hitched them to wagons to pull a heavy load. They saddled the horses when they needed transportation.

The horses of the West were in demand by cowboys, too. While mounted on horseback, the cowboys moved huge herds of cattle to cities where the cattle could be sold for beef. On these long cattle drives, the horses had to endure heat, rain, and winter storms. The cattle drives would never have been possible without dependable, hard-working horses.

No Special Horse

Early horse breeders in the United States were more interested in the strength and shape of a horse than its color. To them, the Palomino horse was no more valuable than any other type of horse.

Although many horses have brown or tan coats, Palominos also possess white manes and tails.

Many Native Americans, however, liked horses with interesting colors. They liked the pattern of light and dark areas on Pintos and the spotted patterns of Appaloosas. They liked Palominos, too. One **Comanche** chief named Quanah Parker owned several Palominos. He said they were smarter and faster than other horses he had ridden.

By the beginning of the 1900s, some horse breeders in the western United States became interested in Palominos. The breeders may have realized that the Palomino pattern was more rare than other colors.

A few breeders worked with Palominos and produced some beautiful horses. Ranchers used many of these Palominos for tending cattle. Other Palominos caught people's attention at races and at horse shows.

A Mysterious Name

Just as no one is sure where the Palomino's unique color came from, no one knows how it got its name. At one time, in fact, these horses had different names in different regions.

Texans called them "yaller" (yellow) horses. In the Midwest, they were "claybanks," because their color matched the clay of some

A Palomino may give birth to a non-Palomino horse.

river banks. In the South, a Palomino was a "gilt," which is another word for "gold." In Missouri, where people always used their best or flashiest horses to drive to church, Palominos were known as "Sunday horses."

Some people say the name "Palomino" is similar to two Spanish words—one for a type of golden grape, and the other for a white dove. Others believe a man with the last name of Palomino might have been one of the first to own a golden horse in America. One historian says that the word can be a Spanish term for "a yellow-stained shirt." There are many possibilities, but no one is completely sure. The mystery of the Palomino name may never be solved.

Chapter 4

What is a Palomino?

For every breed of horse, there are certain guidelines that tell how tall and how heavy the horse should be. Each breed has certain features that all the horses of that breed have in common.

The Palomino is different. It is a color pattern, not a breed. There are Palomino Quarter Horses, Palomino Saddlebreds, and Palomino Arabians.

A Palomino's Color

There are two official organizations that keep track of Palominos. The Palomino Horse Association (PHA) began in 1935. The Palomino Horse Breeders of America (PHBA) was founded six years later, in 1941. These

This dark-brown horse has given birth to a light tan Palomino.

groups have kept records of all Palominos born in the United States and Canada.

Both organizations have certain requirements that a Palomino must meet. The most important is color. A Palomino's coat, they say, must be the color of a newly minted gold coin. (Since the United States no longer mints gold coins, this is somewhat old-fashioned.) Some Palominos will be a little darker and some a little lighter. But the ideal look for a Palomino is shiny gold.

The best Palomino would have no **dapples** (small white patches) on its coat. A Palomino is allowed to have white markings on its face. It may have white on its legs, too, although not above the knees.

The Palomino's Mane and Tail

The mane and tail of a Palomino should be as close to pure white as possible. The PHBA and the PHA allow ivory and silver tails. According to both organizations, a true

Palomino has no more than 15 percent of dark hairs mingled with the white hairs of its tail.

Some horse breeders have been too eager to have their horses registered as Palominos. They have dyed the dark hairs on the horses' manes and tails, so that they look pure white. This is not allowed by the Palomino organizations.

Other Rules

The eyes of Palominos must be black, dark brown, or hazel. They should never be blue. A Palomino cannot be registered if it has dark stripes on its back or zebra stripes on its legs. Some modern horses carry these markings, which have been handed down from ancient horses.

"Foals are rarely born with Palomino color," says one horse owner. "They might be white or beige at first, with dark blue eyes. Over a year or two, the Palomino coloring may come out. But it's always a surprise. Even the eyes of a horse can change color, from dark blue to hazel."

A young horse-lover takes a Palomino colt out for a stroll.

Because of this, the Palomino organizations do not register a horse until it is two years old. By that time, if a horse is going to become the color of a shiny gold coin, it will have done so.

Chapter 5

Palominos in Action

There are many ways people enjoy Palominos today. Some people who own Palominos use them for pleasure riding. Others ride their Palominos in races or enter them in competitions. Some use these golden horses to herd cattle, as their ancestors did. There are other uses for the Palomino that bring these special horses more attention.

This young horse may well be a Palomino. But Palominos can't be officially registered until they are two years old.

Palominos in the Movies

Their striking color has landed many Palominos parts in movies and on television shows. Many Hollywood cowboys have ridden Palominos. The most famous of all such horses was Trigger, ridden by the cowboy star Roy Rogers.

Trigger first began training for the movies in 1937, when he was purchased at an auction. Roy Rogers knew he was a smart horse. But no one ever expected Trigger to learn as much as he did!

Trigger could do more than fifty tricks. He could knock on a door, walk on his hind legs, and untie ropes. He could take a gun out of a bad guy's holster. He could hold one end of a jumprope and twirl it. He could even lie down and cover himself up with a blanket!

Sometimes Roy and Trigger made personal appearances, visiting children in the hospital or doing shows in small and large towns. Kids loved Trigger and many would try to get a souvenir. Sometimes they would snip little pieces from Trigger's tail and mane. Movie schedules often had to be delayed until the raggedy parts grew back.

There were several different Triggers. When one got too old to act in movies, another took his place. Each one was smart, but experts say that none was as great as the original Trigger.

Palominos on Parade

Palominos are a thrilling sight when used as parade horses. There are several Palomino parade groups in the United States and Canada. The horses all have gleaming golden coats, and their riders are all dressed alike.

"We saw a drill team called the Palomino Patrol in a parade last year," says one woman. "They were amazing! The horses kept in rhythm, and not one of them took a step without the others doing it, too. At one point, the horses turned sideways and sidestepped together for almost a block!"

Some of the riders in these drill teams use very fancy equipment. In the western United

States, parade riders use **stirrups** and **saddles**
heavy with silver and gold. One man from
Texas has a saddle with pictures of
stagecoaches, Native American chiefs, and
running horses. The saddle is so heavy that it
has to be lifted onto the Palomino by two men!

Many of the outfits the riders wear are
heavy with gold and silver. There are vests and
hats made of silver, and they glitter with jewels.

Most Palominos are friendly and gentle horses.

One outfit is said to be worth more than $200,000!

"Only a Palomino could hold his own with so much silver and gold on top of him," laughs one horse expert. "No one would dare to put such beautiful jewelry on any other horse!"

More Precious than Gold

The Palomino is a horse of mystery. No one is certain of its origins. No one knows just how it got its name. No one even knows how to predict when a new Palomino will be born!

One thing that is not a mystery is the fact that these are special horses. They are unlike any other horse.

"I love Palominos more than any kind of horse," says one breeder. "I have had seventeen in my life, and I never get tired of looking at them. For me, Palomino gold is more precious than the real kind!"

Glossary

Achilles—an ancient Greek hero who had two magical horses.

Appaloosa—a breed of horse that has one of different color patterns as well as spots

Comanche–a Native American tribe that lived in the southwestern United States

dapples—small white spots on a horse's coat

draft horses—large, muscular horses used for pulling heavy loads

foal—a young horse

gilt—another word for "gold"

hands–four-inch segments, used to measure the height of a horse

pinto–a horse whose coat is made up of large splashes of color

saddles–leather seats used by horse riders

stagecoaches–horse-drawn cars that transported people and goods from place to place. New horses replaced tired ones at each "stage," or station.

stirrups–small metal supports for the feet of horse riders

tapestry–a woven cloth embroidered with pictures or designs

To Learn More

Balch, Glenn. *The Book of Horses.* New York: Four Winds Press, 1967.

Brown, Fern G. *Horses and Foals.* New York: Franklin Watts, 1986.

Clutton-Brock, Juliet. *Horse* (Eyewitness Books). New York: Alfred A.Knopf, 1992.

Henry, Marguerite. *Album of Horses.* New York: Rand McNally, 1951.

Self, Margaret Cabell. *The Complete Book of Horses and Ponies.* New York: McGraw-Hill, 1963.

Some Useful Addresses

Palomino Horse Association
PO Box 324
Jefferson City, MO 65102

Palomino Horse Breeeders of America
15253 E. Skelly Dr.
Tulsa, OK 74116

**National Cowboy Hall of Fame and Rodeo
    Hall of Fame**
1700 NE 63rd St.
Oklahoma City, OK 73113

National Cutting Horse Association
#630-800-6 Avenue SW
Calgary, AB T2P 3G3

Index